Contents

Introduction

If you are wild about learning and wild about animals – this book is for you!

It will take you on a wild adventure, where you will practise key reading comprehension skills and explore the amazing world of animals along the way.

Each reading comprehension topic is introduced in a clear and simple way with lots of interesting activities to complete so that you can practise what you have learned.

Alongside every reading comprehension topic, you will uncover fascinating facts about the world's fastest and slowest animals.

When you have completed each topic, record the animals that you have seen and the skills that you have learned in the explorer's logbook on pages 28–29.

Good luck, explorer!

Rachel Grant

Reading pictures

A

B

C

FACT FILE

Animal: Seahorse
I live in: Shallow warm waters
I weigh: 3–5 g
I eat: Tiny fish and plankton

Task 1	Look at the pictures. Draw lines to match the animals to their names.

Tilly Turtle   **Ollie Octopus**   **Samir Seahorse**

Task 2

We can use pictures to say what happens in a story. Look at the pictures on page 2, labelled A, B and C. Write the correct letter in the answer box to match the sentence to the picture.

They call to Samir, 'Come and play with us!'

☐

Ollie Octopus and Tilly Turtle are friends. They like to swim fast and play with the fishes.

☐

Samir Seahorse watches them play. He can't swim fast. He feels shy.

☐

Task 3

Look at the picture. Write a sentence to show what you think happens next.

_____

_____

_____

_____

WILD FACT

Seahorses can look forwards and backwards at the same time.

WILD FACT

Baby seahorses are very hungry. They eat 3000 pieces of food each day.

Now swim to pages 28–29 to record what you have learned in your explorer's logbook.

More reading pictures

FACT FILE

Animal: Cheetah
I live in: Grasslands and deserts
I weigh: 23–56 kg
I eat: Wildebeest, zebras, deer and antelopes

WILD FACT

When they are happy, cheetahs purr – just like pet cats!

| Task 1 | We can use pictures to find information. Match the labels to the correct pictures. |

cheetah

spots

feet and claws

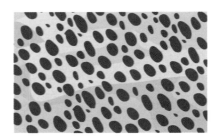

Task 2 Look at the pictures. Circle a picture to answer each question.

a Which animal is faster?

b Which animal has stripes?

c Which animal can roar?

Task 3 Using the Wild Facts and Fact File on pages 4 and 5, write two facts about cheetahs.

_____

_____

_____

_____

WILD FACT

The black lines on a cheetah's face, from its eyes to its mouth, are called tear marks.

Now run to pages 28–29 to record what you have learned in your explorer's logbook.

Reading new words

Task 1 We can use clues to make sense of new words. Look at the picture then circle the correct **bold** word to complete the sentence.

a  Tortoises have **(fur / scales / holes)** all over their skin.

b  Baby tortoises **(hatch / swim / jump)** out of eggs.

c  Tortoises don't have any **(eyes / teeth / legs)**.

Task 2 Read the sentences. Circle the words that explain what the bold word means.

a If a tortoise is **frightened**, it pulls its legs and head inside its shell.

brave / scared / happy

b A tortoise cannot leave its shell. It **carries** its home wherever it goes.

takes / lives / leaves

c The tortoise's hard shell **protects** it from enemies.

slows down / keeps safe / makes small

d Tortoises' shells come in many **different** colours. Some are grey. Some are brown.

bright / not the same / beautiful

WILD FACT

Tortoises have strong mouths, but no teeth.

Task 3 Terry the tortoise feels grumpy today. Draw his face.

WILD FACT

Although it has a hard shell, a tortoise can still feel when you touch it.

Now stroll to pages 28–29 to record what you have learned in your explorer's logbook.

Telling stories

We can use pictures to tell a story. Draw lines to match the sentences to the pictures.

He can't catch them. The birds always fly away.

Flash loves to run fast. His favourite game is chasing pigeons.

Flash wishes he could fly too.

FACT FILE

Animal: Greyhound
I live in: Human homes, because I am a pet
I weigh: 29–31 kg
I eat: Meat, vegetables, fruit and dry dog food

WILD FACT

Although they run very fast, greyhounds are quite lazy. They can sleep up to 18 hours each day!

Task 2

Look at the pictures. Number the sentences so that they tell the story. The first one has been done for you.

1

2

3

4

a Flash was running so fast that he couldn't stop.   ___3___

b One day, Flash decided to chase pigeons. He sprinted across the field.   _____

c Suddenly, his feet left the ground. 'I'm flying!' he thought.   _____

d As usual, all the birds flew up.   _____

Task 3

What do you think happened next? Write one sentence of your own to finish the story in Task 2.

_____

_____

_____

_____

WILD FACT

Greyhounds have special eyesight that helps them see moving objects up to 800 metres away.

Now sprint to pages 28–29 to record what you have learned in your explorer's logbook.

Reading rhymes

Some words have similar sounds when we say them. These are called rhymes. Rhymes are often used in poems.

FACT FILE

Animal: Snail
I live in: Dark damp soil, trees, plants and rocks
I weigh: 12 g
I eat: Plants, fruits, vegetables and algae

Task 1   Circle one word that rhymes with the word in bold.

a **snail**	wall	smile	trail
b **slow**	flew	grow	cow
c **slide**	glide	spade	buy
d **foot**	hand	put	take
e **shell**	wide	cart	bell
f **rock**	clock	brick	talk

Circle the rhymes in the poem, then answer the questions by underlining the correct answer.

A snail with his shell
Has his home on his back.
His foot and its slime
Leave a silvery track.

For all that he's slow,
He makes his own way.
Up walls he can slide –
But it takes him all day!

a What leaves a silvery track?   **shell**   **slide**   **slime**

b Where can a snail slide?   **own way**   **up walls**   **all day**

Task 3   Find and write words in the poem in task 2 that rhyme with the words below.

a toe _____   **b** climb _____   **c** bell _____

d roam _____   **e** takes _____   **f** hay _____

WILD FACT

A snail has one very strong foot. The foot makes slime so it can slide up sticks, stalks and walls.

WILD FACT

Although many of them live on land, snails are actually a kind of shellfish.

Now slide to pages 28–29 to record what you have learned in your explorer's logbook.

Reading stories

FACT FILE

Animal: Hare
I live in: Open farmland
I weigh: 2.5–6.5 kg
I eat: Grass, ferns, twigs and buds

Stories have a beginning, a middle and an end. Fairy stories and fables often use the same words and phrases.

Task 1 Draw lines to show where you would find these phrases in a story.

a They all lived happily ever after   At the beginning

b Then, one day   In the middle

c Once upon a time   At the end

Task 2 Write the title of the story where you would find the phrases.

a 'Fee, fi, fo, fum!'

_____

_____

WILD FACT

Hares can travel three metres in one leap – that's a long way!

b 'Granny, what big ears you have!'

_____

_____

Task 3   Read the story.

1

2

3

4

Use words from the box to answer the questions.

asleep	slow	faster

a The hare was _____ than the tortoise.

b The hare lost the race because
he fell _____.

c The tortoise won because he was
_____ and steady.

WILD FACT

Male hares fight each other by standing on their back legs as if they are boxing.

Now leap to pages 28–29 to record what you have
learned in your explorer's logbook.

Reading instructions

Starfish have one eye at the tip of each of their arms.

Instructions tell us how to do or make something. They tell us what to do in the right order. We can use instructions to learn how to make something (like a sandwich) or how to play something (like a game).

Task 1 Copy the correct answer from the box.

facts	how to do or make things	a story

Instructions tell us _____.

Task 2 Which of these is the title for a book of instructions? Tick ✓ one.

The Silly Starfish ☐

How to Make a Starfish ☐

Starfish Facts ☐

FACT FILE

Animal: Starfish
I live in: Oceans and seas
I weigh: Up to 5 kg
I eat: Clams, shells and mussels

Task 3 Read these instructions.

You will need:

a paper plate   a pen   glue

a pair of scissors   paints   glitter or beads

1 Draw five arms for the starfish shape on the back of the paper plate.

2 Cut out the starfish shape carefully.

3 Paint it in a bright colour.

4 Put glue down the centre of each leg.

5 Sprinkle the legs with glitter or stick beads on to the glue.

Now use words from the box to answer the questions.

a pen	one	to stick glitter or beads	five

a How many paper plates do you need? _____

b How many arms does the starfish have? _____

c What do you use to draw the shape? _____

d Why do you need glue? _____

Tick ✓ the sentence that is **true**. Cross ✗ the sentence that is **false**.

e You need to sprinkle glitter before you put the glue on the legs. ☐

f You should use paint that is a bright colour. ☐

WILD FACT

Starfish have tiny tube feet to help them move along the sea bed.

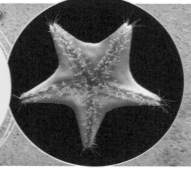

Now walk to pages 28–29 to record what you have learned in your explorer's logbook.

Reading play scripts

WILD FACT

Peregrine falcons catch prey by diving very fast through the air. The fastest dive ever recorded is 389 km per hour – faster than a sports car!

FACT FILE

Animal: Peregrine falcon
I live in: Mountains and cliffs
I weigh: 0.5–1.6 kg
I eat: Birds and small animals

Play scripts tell stories through the words each character says. These words come after the name of the character that is speaking.

character's name

Falcon   I'm the fastest bird in the sky!

words the character says

Task 1
Write words on the lines to complete the sentences.

a Play scripts tell _____.

b Next to each character's name, you will find _____ he or she says.

Task 2   Read this play script.

One beautiful, sunny day, Baby Falcon decides to have some fun with the other birds.

Baby Falcon   I'm the fastest bird in the sky! Whee!

Pigeon   I bet I can catch you.

Baby Falcon   Swoop, swoop as fast as you can. You can't catch me, for I'm a falcon!

Baby Falcon swoops past Pigeon.

Swallow   I'm a fast flyer. I will catch you.

Baby Falcon   Dive, dive as fast as you can. You can't catch me, for I'm a falcon!

Baby Falcon dives past Swallow.
Suddenly, Baby Falcon feels a whoosh! Something swoops past him.

Baby Falcon   Oops! Oh, hello Mum!

Mrs Falcon   Playtime is over, son. Let's go home.

Now draw a line to match the beginning of each sentence with its correct ending.

a Baby Falcon swoops   faster than her son.

b Baby Falcon dives   is a fast flyer.

c Swallow thinks he   past Pigeon.

d Mrs Falcon flies   past Swallow.

WILD FACT

Falcons have three eyelids. The third eyelid protects their eyes when they dive.

Task 3   Answer these questions about the play script in Task 2.

a How do you think Baby Falcon feels when his mum arrives?

_____

b Which word tells you that Baby Falcon is enjoying himself?

_____

Now swoop to pages 28–29 to record what you have learned in your explorer's logbook.

Using a dictionary

FACT FILE
Animal: Koala
I live in: Trees
I weigh: 9–14 kg
I eat: Eucalyptus leaves

WILD FACT

Koalas have fingerprints, just like humans.

A dictionary is a book that has lots of words with their meanings. The words are in alphabetical order. For example:

apple   comes before   **art**
because 'p' comes before 'r' in the alphabet.

Use a dictionary:
- when you don't know the meaning of a word
- when you need to check the spelling of a word.

knock	to hit something quickly and hard
knot	1) something that is tied tightly together and is difficult to undo
	2) to tie something together
know	to understand information
knowledge	information and facts
koala	an Australian animal with grey fur and round ears

label	a small piece of paper or cloth with information on it
lace	1) a string that holds things together
	2) a pretty cloth made of threads knotted in a pattern
ladder	two long pieces of metal or wood with steps in between
lady	another word for a woman

Task 1   Look at the dictionary pages. Write the word for each meaning.

a pretty cloth made of knotted threads   _____

b information and facts   _____

c a furry animal from Australia   _____

Task 2 If you were to add these words to the dictionary, which word would each one come after?

a knuckle _____

b ladle _____

Task 3 Look at the dictionary pages, then answer the questions.

a Which word means 'to understand information'?

_____

b Which word comes after the word 'knowledge'?

_____

Task 4 Write two meanings for this word. Use a dictionary to check your answer.

tear 1) _____

2) _____

WILD FACT

Koalas talk to each other by making a noise called a 'bellow', which sounds like a snore.

Now climb to pages 28–29 to record what you have learned in your explorer's logbook.

Reading non-fiction

Non-fiction writing gives us information or facts. It can tell us about real things, including things that happened in the past. It may tell us:

- when something happened
- where or why it happened
- who was involved.

FACT FILE

Animal:	Sailfish
I live in:	The oceans
I weigh:	54–100 kg
I eat:	Small fish, squid, octopus

WILD FACT

Sailfish flatten the fin on their back when they need to swim fast.

POST CARD

Dear Nanny and Granddad

We are having a great time. There are many amazing animals here. I saw sloths and monkeys in the hotel gardens.

Yesterday we went on a fishing trip. Dad helped me with the rod. First, Maya caught a small fish. Then we caught a sailfish! We were very excited because sailfish are the fastest fish. Don't worry, we let them go free.

I also saw sea turtles and pelicans.

Lots of love,

Tommy

COSTA RICA

Mr and Mrs Drew

22 Hillrise

Glasgow

G22 0BR

UK

Task 1 Look at the postcard and answer the questions.

a What country is Tommy in? _____

b Who is Tommy writing to? _____

20

Task 2   Now answer these questions about the postcard on page 20.

a What animals did Tommy see at the hotel?

He saw _____

b What did they do yesterday?

They _____

c Who went fishing?

_____ went fishing.

d What is special about sailfish?

_____

Task 3   Write two questions to ask Tommy when he comes home. Use two of the words in the box. Remember to use punctuation.

| who   when   where   what   why |

1 _____

2 _____

Now glide to pages 28–29 to record what you have
learned in your explorer's logbook.

Reading characters

A character is someone who does things in stories. You may learn about a character's actions, thoughts or feelings. You may learn more about a character from the things he or she says.

Task 1 Look at the picture, then answer the questions.

a What do you think the sloth is feeling?

_____

b What is the sloth thinking? Write it in the thought bubble.

FACT FILE

Animal: Sloth
I live in: Trees in the jungle
I weigh: 3–6 kg
I eat: Leaves, buds, twigs and fruit

WILD FACT

Sloths spend most of their time hanging upside down!

Task 2 Look at the picture,
then answer the questions.

WILD FACT

Sloths are
clumsy on land
but they are great
swimmers!

Why do you scurry around all day?
You should slow down
and take it easy.

I have a family to feed.
I can't hang around
all day, like you!

a What advice does the sloth give to the mouse?

_____

b Why does the mouse scurry around?

_____

c Decide which words describe each character. Write them in the
correct place in the table below.

lazy   cross   energetic   curious   hard-working
friendly   thoughtful   calm   active   busy

Sloth	Mouse

Task 3 Choose one word that you wrote in task 2c. Explain why
the word describes the character.

_____

_____

**Now climb to pages 28–29 to record what you have
learned in your explorer's logbook.**

Reading poems

Poems can tell us about feelings or ideas. They often use rhymes and rhythm.

Rhymes are words that sound similar when you say them.

Rhythm is the beat of the words that you can hear as you say them.

WILD FACT

Squirrels can smell food that is buried, even if it is under snow.

Task 1

Read these lines from a poem aloud. Mark where you hear a beat. The first line has been done for you.

Oh! <u>Fris</u>ky <u>squi</u>rrels <u>scur</u>rying <u>through</u> the <u>trees</u>,
On tiny paws with bushy tails you scamper,

FACT FILE

Animal: Squirrel
I live in: Woods, forests and parks
I weigh: 400–600 g
I eat: Acorns, nuts, berries and seeds

WILD FACT

A squirrel's front teeth never stop growing, which is useful for gnawing on hard nuts.

Task 2 Read this poem, then answer the questions.

Oh! Frisky squirrels scurrying through the trees,
On tiny paws with bushy tails you scamper,
All grey and silver fur, with skilful ease
Collecting nuts to fill your winter hamper!

a Why are the squirrels collecting nuts?

_____

b Find **two** words that describe how the squirrels move.

_____

c Which word in the poem rhymes with **scamper**?

_____

d Find **two** words in the poem that rhyme with **please**.

_____

e How many beats can you hear in each line?

_____

f Which **two** words tell you that the poet thinks squirrels are clever?

_____

Task 3 Practise reading the poem in Task 2. First, read it slowly
to yourself twice. Check you can pronounce all the words
correctly.

Look carefully at the punctuation marks. The commas tell you to pause.
The exclamation marks tell you about the feelings of the narrator (the
person telling the story).

When you are ready, take a big breath. Read the poem out loud as
clearly as you can.

Now scamper to pages 28–29 to record what you have
learned in your explorer's logbook.

Quick test

Now try these questions. Give yourself 1 mark for every correct answer.

1 **Draw a picture to show what you think happens next.**

2 **Look at the weather chart, then circle the answers to the questions.**

	Monday	Tuesday	Wednesday	Thursday	Friday
a.m.	☀	☀	🌧	🌧	❄
p.m.	🌧	☀	☀	🌧	❄

a Did it rain on Wednesday afternoon?   **Yes**   **No**

b Which day was best for a trip to the beach?   **Tuesday**   **Thursday**

c Which was the coldest day?   **Monday**   **Friday**

3 *If you throw a ball for our dog, she will <u>fetch</u> it back.*
What does the word fetch mean? Circle one answer.

catch / bring / take

4 Put the pictures in order. Label them 1, 2 and 3.

5 Circle one word that rhymes with the bold word.

ring   dig   thing   rain

6 Put a ✓ where you would expect to find these sentences in a story.

	In the middle	At the end
They were all very glad to be home again.		
'Look out!' cried Althea.		

7 Tick ✓ the sentence that is true.

Instructions tell us a story. ☐

Instructions tell us how to do or make something. ☐

8 Underline the words that the character says.

Pigeon   I bet I can catch you.

9 Put these words in the order you will find them in a dictionary. The first one has been done for you.

thirsty   think   thanks   three

thanks   _____   _____   _____

10 Copy one word to complete the sentence below.

funny   real   made-up

Non-fiction writing can tell us about _____ things and things that happened in the past.

11 Draw lines to match each word to the correct definition.

rhythm   tells us about feelings or ideas

poem   words that have similar sounds

rhyme   the beat of the words as you say them

How did you do? 1–3 Try again!   4–7 Good try!   / 13
8–10 Great work!   11–13 Excellent exploring!

Explorer's Logbook

Tick off the topics as you complete them and then colour in the star.

Reading pictures ☐

More reading pictures ☐

Reading new words ☐

Telling stories ☐

Reading rhymes ☐

Reading stories ☐

Reading instructions ☐

Reading play scripts ☐

Using a dictionary ☐

Reading non-fiction ☐

Reading characters ☐

Reading poems ☐

Answers

Pages 2–3
Task 1

Tilly Turtle   Ollie Octopus   Samir Seahorse

Task 2

They call to Samir, 'Come and play with us!'   **C**

Ollie Octopus and Tilly Turtle are friends. They like
to swim fast and play with the fishes.   **A**

Samir Seahorse watches them play. He can't swim fast.
He feels shy.   **B**

Task 3

Child's own sentence that makes sense in the story,
e.g. Ollie, Samir and Tilly all play together and have fun
with the fishes.

Pages 4–5
Task 1

 – cheetah   – spots

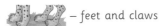 – feet and claws

Task 2

 a   **b**   **c**

Task 3

Child's own answers, in sentences that make sense,
e.g. A cheetah purrs when it is happy. Cheetahs live in
grasslands and deserts.

Pages 6–7
Task 1

a scales   **b** hatch   **c** teeth

Task 2

a scared   **b** takes   **c** keeps safe

d not the same

Task 3

The child should draw a tortoise's face that looks grumpy
and bad-tempered.

Pages 8–9
Task 1

 Flash loves to run fast. His favourite game is
chasing pigeons.

 He can't catch them. The birds always fly away.

 Flash wishes he could fly too.

Task 2

a 3   **b** 1   **c** 4   **d** 2

Task 3

Child's own answer, in a sentence that makes sense in the
story, e.g. Flash fell back to the ground, because he can't
really fly.

Pages 10–11
Task 1

a trail   **b** grow   **c** glide

d put   **e** bell   **f** clock

Task 2

Rhymes: back / track; day / way

a slime   **b** up walls

Task 3

a slow   **b** slime   **c** shell

d home   **e** makes   **f** day

Pages 12–13
Task 1

a At the end   **b** In the middle   **c** At the beginning

Task 2

a Jack and the Beanstalk   **b** Red Riding Hood

Task 3

a faster   **b** asleep   **c** slow

Pages 14–15
Task 1

how to do or make things

Task 2

How to Make a Starfish   ✓

Task 3

a one   **b** five   **c** a pen

d to stick glitter or beads

e You need to sprinkle glitter before you put the
glue on the legs.   ✗

f You should use paint that is a bright colour.   ✓

Pages 16–17
Task 1

a stories   **b** the words

Task 2

a Baby Falcon swoops past Pigeon.

b Baby Falcon dives past Swallow.

c Swallow thinks he is a fast flyer.

d Mrs Falcon flies faster than her son.

Task 3

a Child's own answer, based on the play script, e.g.
surprised, embarrassed.

b Whee!

Pages 18–19

Task 1

a lace **b** knowledge **c** koala

Task 2

a knowledge **b** ladder

Task 3

a know **b** koala

Task 4

Two from: to rip or pull apart into pieces / a drop of liquid that comes from the eye / to rush, hurry

Pages 20–21

Task 1

a Costa Rica (the stamp tells you this)

b His Nanny and Granddad/ Mr and Mrs Drew

Task 2

a He saw sloths and monkeys.

b They went fishing / went on a fishing trip.

c Tommy, Dad and Maya went fishing.

d Sailfish are the fastest fish.

Task 3

Child's own questions. Ensure that each question starts with a capital letter and ends with a question mark. Each question must start with a 'w' word. Examples: When did you get back from Costa Rica? What was the best thing about your holiday?

Pages 22–23

Task 1

a Child's own answer, e.g. sleepy

b Child's own answer, e.g. What's happening?

Task 2

a Slow down and take it easy.

b Because it has a family to feed.

c

Sloth	Mouse
lazy	cross
curious	energetic
calm	hard-working
thoughtful	active
friendly	busy

Task 3

Child's own answer. Look for an explanation that relates to the conversation, e.g. The mouse is hard-working because it says it needs to find food for its family / The sloth is curious because it asks the mouse a question.

Pages 24–25

Task 1

On <u>tiny</u> <u>paws</u> with <u>bushy</u> <u>tails</u> you <u>scamper</u>.

Task 2

a to store for the winter ('winter hamper')

b scamper, scurrying

c hamper

d trees, ease

e 5

f skilful ease

Task 3

Child should read clearly, with correct emphasis.

Pages 26–27

1 Child's own picture that makes sense, e.g. a sunflower growing from the pot.

2 a No **b** Tuesday **c** Friday

3 bring

4

 2   3   1

5 thing

6

	In the middle	At the end
They were all very glad to be home again.		✓
'Look out!' cried Althea.	✓	

7 Instructions tell us how to do or make something

8 <u>I bet I can catch you</u>.

9 thanks, think, thirsty, three

10 real

11 rhythm – the beat of the words as you say them

poem – tells us about feelings or ideas

rhyme – words that have similar sounds

Well done, explorer!

You have finished your reading comprehension adventure!

Explorer's pass

Name: _____

Age: _____

Date: _____

Draw a picture of yourself in the box!